D1712125

FAMOUS U.S. SONGS

By Charlotte Taylor

DISCOVER!

Enslow
PUBLISHING

Please visit our website, www.enslow.com. For a free color catalog of all our high-quality books, call toll free 1-800-398-2504 or fax 1-877-980-4454.

Library of Congress Cataloging-in-Publication Data

Names: Taylor, Charlotte, 1978– author.
Title: Famous U.S. songs / Charlotte Taylor.
Description: New York : Enslow Publishing, 2021. | Series: Being a U.S. citizen | Includes index.
Identifiers: LCCN 2019054530 | ISBN 9781978517493 (library binding) | ISBN 9781978517479 (paperback) | ISBN 9781978517486 (6 Pack) | ISBN 9781978517509 (ebook)
Subjects: LCSH: Patriotic songs—United States—History and criticism—Juvenile literature. | National songs—United States—History and criticism—Juvenile literature.
Classification: LCC ML3561.P37 T38 2020 | DDC 782.42/15990973—dc23
LC record available at https://lccn.loc.gov/2019054530

Published in 2021 by
Enslow Publishing
101 West 23rd Street, Suite #240
New York, NY 10011

Designer: Laura Bowen
Editor: Megan Quick

Photo credits: Cover, pp. 1, 18 (instruments) Rakshenko Ekaterina/Shutterstock.com; cover, pp. 1, 6, 8, 10, 14, 16, 20 (kids, music notes) ann131313/Shutterstock.com; p. 4 Alexander Ryabintsev/Shutterstock.com; p. 5 Daisy-Daisy/iStock.com; p. 7 Bettmann/Contributor/Bettmann/Getty Images; p. 9 Leonard Zhukovsky/Shutterstock.com; p. 11 Ariel Skelley/DigitalVision/Getty Images; p. 12 Sudowoodo/Shutterstock.com; p. 13 New York Times Co./Contributor/Archive Photos/Getty Images; p. 15 PhotoEnglish/Shutterstock.com; p. 17 MahirAtes/iStock.com; p. 19 ClassicStock/Contributor/Archive Photos/Getty Images; p. 21 Ariel Skelley/DigitalVision/Getty Images.

Portions of this work were originally authored by Harriet Wesolowski and published as *The Songs We Sing: Honoring Our Country*. All new material in this edition was authored by Charlotte Taylor.

Printed in the United States of America

Some of the images in this book illustrate individuals who are models. The depictions do not imply actual situations or events.

CPSIA compliance information: Batch #BS20ENS: For further information contact Enslow Publishing, New York, New York, at 1-800-398-2504.

Find us on

CONTENTS

Boldface words appear in Words to Know.

CELEBRATING AMERICA

People love to sing songs about America. They are proud of their country. There are songs about our history, people, and places. Some of the most famous songs are about the American flag. These songs **celebrate** what is special about our country.

SOME SONGS ABOUT AMERICA ARE VERY OLD, AND SOME ARE NEW.

AMERICA'S SONG

"The Star-Spangled Banner" is our **national anthem**. It's our country's **official** song. It's about the American flag. Francis Scott Key wrote the song in 1814 during a war. There was a big battle. When it ended, Key saw our flag. It looked beautiful.

THE AMERICAN FLAG STILL FLEW AFTER THE BATTLE. IT SHOWED THAT AMERICA WAS STRONG.

7

In our national anthem, the flag is a **symbol** of America. It means that our country is free and Americans are brave. We sing the song to honor our country. We sing it at special **events**. You may even sing it at school.

THE NATIONAL ANTHEM TELLS ABOUT THE STARS AND STRIPES ON OUR FLAG.

9

FLY THE FLAG

"You're a Grand Old Flag" is another song about our flag. George M. Cohan wrote the song for a play that came out in 1906. People liked the play. They liked the song even more! It's a good marching song.

"YOU'RE A GRAND OLD FLAG" HAS A HAPPY TUNE AND A STRONG BEAT.

Cohan wrote his song after he met a **soldier**. The soldier carried around an old American flag. He loved his country. He told Cohan the flag was a "grand old rag." Cohan changed the word "rag" to "flag" for his song.

GEORGE M. COHAN WROTE LOTS OF POPULAR SONGS AND PLAYS.

GEORGE M. COHAN

FROM SEA TO SHINING SEA

"America the Beautiful" is a famous song about our country. It was a **poem** first printed in 1895. Katharine Lee Bates wrote the words after she went up a mountain and saw the beautiful view. Samuel Ward wrote the music in 1882.

KATHARINE BATES WROTE HER POEM AFTER SHE CLIMBED THIS MOUNTAIN IN COLORADO.

PIKES PEAK

Katharine Bates traveled a lot. In her song, she wrote about the different parts of America. She wrote about green fields and blue skies. She wrote about tall, purple mountains. Her song also says that Americans are brave and free.

"AMBER WAVES OF GRAIN" ARE THE WHEAT FIELDS IN MANY PARTS OF AMERICA.

PROUD TO BE A YANKEE

Many little children sing "Yankee Doodle."
It was first sung hundreds of years ago.
Americans wanted to be free from the
British. The two sides went to war.
The British soldiers sang "Yankee
Doodle" to make fun of
the Americans.

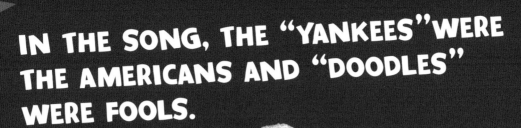

IN THE SONG, THE "YANKEES" WERE THE AMERICANS AND "DOODLES" WERE FOOLS.

American soldiers decided they liked "Yankee Doodle." They were proud to be Yankees! They changed some of the words and made it their own song. It's a funny song. It's also about being proud to be an American.

"YANKEE DOODLE" IS OFTEN PLAYED ON THE FOURTH OF JULY.

WORDS TO KNOW

celebrate To honor with special activities.

event Something important that happens.

national anthem The official song of a country.

official Having the support of a group.

poem A piece of writing with special language and rhythm.

soldier A person in the armed forces.

symbol Something that stands for something else.

FOR MORE INFORMATION

Books

Ferguson, Melissa Ann. *American Symbols: What You Need to Know.* North Mankato, MN: Capstone Press, 2017.

Hartland, Jessie. *Our Flag Was Still There: The True Story of Mary Pickersgill and the Star-Spangled Banner.* New York, NY: Simon & Schuster, 2019.

Websites

Patriotic Songs

kids.niehs.nih.gov/games/songs/patriotic/index.htm
Learn the words and listen to the tunes of U.S. songs.

You're a Grand Old Flag

bussongs.com/songs/grand-old-flag
Enjoy the patriotic video and music of this popular song.

INDEX